LOTUS

LOTUS
कमल

arjun thakrar

ISBN: 9798702425405

the way to truth is through ahimsa

-   Gandhi

Dear Reader,

I think before you go into this book, it may be beneficial for me to explain a little about its contents and my journey in writing these poems.

Poems and essays are types of writing that I have been sporadically penning since around 2014. Whenever there has been a development in my life, either physical or emotional, I often feel the desire to write about it. When there is a moment, delicate or abrasive, I often feel the need to transcribe it. Or, sometimes, current issues or affairs drive me to write essays, that still lie tucked away in the locked folders of my laptop.

This book contains none of that – in part, simply because I have not yet experienced enough of life for there to be enough to form a collection worth sharing. This book, instead, shares with you a different journey. A type of self-discovery that travels back to the roots of my existence.

You see, it was in 2017 that I decided I was going to discover more about where I came from. India and Hinduism, being so rich and so deep, have always been things that I can read about for hours on end with rapt attention. But in 2017, I found myself intent to explore this further and learn about my cultural and religious identity.

Now do not be mistaken – this is not a book on religion. There will be no preaching present on these pages – just appreciation and exploration.

From youth, I have adored the magical and almost fairytale-like nature of Hinduism. The countless powerful deities and the epic and elaborate stories. From a young age, I can recall being engrossed in watching and reading the Ramayana, and painting my favourite gods, whilst my peers were playing with action-men and painting race cars.

Years and youth passed and, as I have grown, experiencing a few more years of life, I have become more culturally and internationally aware. In my early teens, I became fascinated with India - both its present and the past. Its years of deep and ingrained history, stemming from the oldest civilization on earth. The old tales of the Mahabharata, and the formation of the Indus Valley, from which language, democracy, science, and maths were born. The years when kings ruled, wars waged, and a tapestry of monarchs culminated in a tangible history of unrivalled grandeur and elegance in the form of indo-mughal architecture. I began to form a deeper love and understanding for the colourful traditions and festivals that form my religion; Holi, Diwali, Navratri, and the dances, celebrations, and rituals that accompany them. There even came a point where I shirked my immaturity and began to enjoy the length and depth of Hindu weddings, which in themselves are spectacles of vibrancy, compassion, principle and ritual.

And so, I continued to grow, leaving my late teens behind and beginning the journey into adulthood - where I now live. Where my desire is to not just learn more, but to *understand* more, and has resulted in the creation of the poems that ink these pages.

It was in 2017 that I knew I wanted more; I had already begun to appreciate my religion and understand it in a way that I hadn't before, but I was not satisfied with what I knew. I needed to delve further and understand the principles, beliefs, and legends on a much deeper level.

This book recounts the discoveries of my early adult years: Reading books on the ancient and modern history of individual cities in India, delving into the Bhagavad Gita, the Puranas, and the Upanishads. Learning the lesser-known myths, their deeper moral meanings, and what they teach about living life. Understanding and discovering the core principles of Hindu life; Choice in *Dharma*, Kindness in *Karma*, Peace in *Ahimsa* and Spirituality in *Yoga*. Finding release in adopting Yoga, changing my life to incorporate meditation into my mornings, and understanding the world in the *gunas* of truth, passion and darkness.

That is what this book is. My journey, that has not and will not end. These poems recount my voyage; how it has changed my outlook on the world, what it has taught me about how to live a good and pure life, how it has developed my mindset, and consequentially me.

So whilst these poems may mean nothing to someone else, they mean a lot to me. For me, this collection is almost a time capsule of my steps into the real world. If you take one thing from this book – one guiding principle above all others – take *Ahimsa*. Believe it and live your life by it, for at its core it preaches peace. Live a life filled with peace, kindness, and respect for everything and everyone in every part of your life.

Heart, Hands and Mind

This book is divided into three parts. These sections each represent a distinct Hindu principle, into which most of our life experiences and actions can be sorted.

I want to explain a little about these principles to you before you proceed. Though I caution you not to take my word as gospel – I am no academic or expert in Indology. Instead, I will explain what these terms have come to mean to me, throughout my reading and learning, and in turn how these categories relate to the poems contained within them.

Ahimsa Peace

To me, I understand *Ahimsa* simply as peace. For me, it encapsulates the underpinning principle of how we should approach the world throughout our lives and how we should interact with the people and things around us – the external facet of the world. It is a simple idea that is about peace and respect for all living beings. To other people, we should be kind and forgiving, supportive and true. We should rid ourselves of negative attributes, such as selfishness, jealousy, and anger. A life should be led doing good.

Such respect, I believe, must extend to all living beings, animals included. Such affection should be bestowed upon all, blood should not be shed, and pain not inflicted. And to live a life behaving in such a way is a promise that harmony can be formed; if you go through your life exuding peace and kindness, then kindness and peace will find you.

Dharma Choice

To me *Dharma* is not so much about duty as it is about choice – the choices we make for ourselves. Of course, *Ahimsa* must underpin our decisions, keeping our intentions good and pure, but Dharma is choosing the right path for you. To pursue your ambitions and goals in life, but to also consider your body and mind, choosing actions that will balance both. And these choices should, of course, be the ones that are right for you, but should also consider what is good for others. The choices we make should be true to us and our desires, but should also be choices that help us to achieve these without bringing detriment to others. To use our choices to bring as much good to others as these choices bring to ourselves.

Yoga Spirituality

To me, *Yoga* is about the mind. It sheds all physical aspects of the external world and our outward choices and, instead, focuses internally on us and our mental constitution. The way we feel about ourselves and the internal climate of our mind and soul. Yoga does not concern the world nor any physicality but, instead, the soul. It is about knowing the connection we share with the parts of the world we cannot see and following those invisible threads that link our spirituality and guide us on the journey to *moksha*.

Ahimsa

namaste

every dawn
when the sun glides upwards
you delicately greet the morning
and the day greets your soul

you take your steps
forwards
in that new day
a new chance to live
a new life
with new choices

each choice is a question
but only to yourself
and yet it is not a question
at all

for every action
choice
movement
and emotion
is exactly as it should be

the dance you make
through the new day
is the grace and rhythm
of your divine soul

your divine soul
channelling yoga
as it greets a million others
hands clasped
in recognition

it moves you
in the way you should move
so question no action
but instead
let the moments
when your soul greets another
guide you forwards
for eternity

droplets

teach the world
ahimsa; to be kind

preacher of peace
let the knowledge
belief
trickle down

a drop
in the ocean
can make
a wave

savitri

so good
and pure
was her mind

that even death
could not steal
from her

yama

even the master
of all life

stood down

when
love and wisdom
stared him in the face

nakshatra

it was a heavenly mansion of studded stars
where even under the guise of night
it was not darkness that prevailed
but rather a delicate and glimmering light

where was up and where was down?
did the sky glitter through cracks in the stones?
or did the winding ganga reflect a symphony of
jewels?

if he jumped, would he sink or would he fly?
was he feathers or fins?

the stars could guide him, he knew
but how to choose?

when there were so many diamonds high
above, strung by the slender fingers of the
goddess
how could he choose which one to follow?
which one would lead him through the sky and
down the river?

he had read the stars, many times
weathered and matted, under the banyan
his limber frame clad in saffron
he had spoken to the gems

they always spoke back
sometimes they would tell tales of the future;
of marriage and joy; of death and sadness; of
wars to come and words that would split the
earth

sometimes they would tell tales of the past;
of battles that turned family against family; of
battles that spawned books of knowledge; of
battles that infected humans with energy,
binding them to sticks of wood and charging
them to dance for nine long nights

but now, the stars lay silent
their voices had sifted below even a whisper
no longer did they speak
now they only gazed
they blinded

sita

so true
was she entirely
that even flames
could not burn her

dhasrat

her spite
and greed
and power
broke
his heart
his body
and soul

it was love
that held him
together

and without it
he crumbled

karuna

if you listen you can hear

sometimes it is louder
clear as day

yet sometimes it is quiet
nothing but a whisper
like the hush of night

but everything
all around us
is breathing

from the silent limbs, gnarled and scored
to the gentle flitter of webbed wings
and the kiss of wind, whispering histories

the world is alive
a symphony of breathing
approaching a crescendo

but no, it must not
for if it reaches a peak so loud
then it must begin to fall

after the crescendo
must come the silence
when the breath ceases
and silence falls

no, we must maintain a tremolo
of constant life
with notes only fading
in their natural course

the peace is not in silence
but in the gentle hum
of knowing
that no crescendo
is needed

for the harmony
when filled

with so many beings

is loud

kindness

one should not
seek kindness

for you
should have given it
already

ripple

every good thought
you think
makes you
a little better

every good thought
you speak
make the world
a little better

vasudhaiva kutumbakam

humans
are the only beings
that choose
to love
differently

you see
the elements
they do not
differentiate

they both love
and hate
equally

air loves
unconditionally
feeding life
breathing lungs
of every creature
every leaf
and every petal

and fire burns
indifferently
parting for no being
not for ancient bark
nor the weak or young
it burns all
without remorse

water feeds
without reservation
ushering solstice
and existence
past the lips
and roots
of every atom
that chooses
to breathe

but humans
we are not so giving
and not so pure

humans
we choose
we love some
and not others

we prune roses
but fell trees

we love the canine
but eat the bovine
we pet the fur
before slaughtering
the leather

you see
we do not
love
in equal amounts

nor do we dispense
kindness
in equal measures

whilst all
of nature
treats each other
as equal
humans
can not

and yet
what is power
if you do
not know
how to love

Dharma

dharma

if the world
is cruel

be kind

surya

there was a king
he was the sun

but he shone
too bright
for his love
to bear

so he cut
a piece
of himself
away

and threw it
down
into the ocean
below

and there
it fizzled
and bubbled
and died

the sun
no longer
could shine
as bright

but finally
he could
be with
his queen

with her
he shone
twice as
bright

generosity

can you hear
the sun
rise

the delicate
whisper
as it floats over
the trees

it blazes bright
strong and
powerful

and yet
it is not
selfish

can you feel
the sun?

all it does
is give

hanuman

he carried
the weight
of an entire
mountain

to save
the ones
he loved

where there is a will

there is a way

if the world
is upside down

let the world be

either
the world will right
or you will learn
to walk through the sky

mahishasura

you see
there was a buffalo
strong as mountains
smart as the skies

and he could not
as much as many tried
be defeated

and he cried it so
he would scream from hilltops
from plains and deserts
he would shout
that no man can kill me
no man can destroy me
i am invincible

and he was
no man *could* kill the buffalo
many tried
and many died
for the buffalo
with a sword in one hand
and a snake in the other
would smite down those
who crossed his path

but whilst the buffalo was smart
he was also ignorant
his mind was strong
but not open
his arms were confident
but only of what they knew

for one day
a beauty graced his presence
a lioness
a woman
and he thought nothing of it
she was after all
a woman

and she smiled
neither kindly nor unkindly
but knowingly
for she had heard his cries
that no man
could kill him
and so
the buffalo's eyes
wide with lust
turned wide with surprise

for she slew him
in the same manner
that he had slayed men
with a sharp knife
and a sharp hand
his heart was carved
both apart and out

it was true
no man could kill him
but of course
she was not a man
she was a woman

judgement

the moon seems pure
yet she is scarred

the sun moves slow
yet he is burning

your mind is dark
yet you are glowing
you just cannot see it

open

when he opened
his mind
the shadows
escaped

all that remained
was light

when he opened
his heart
the chains
of apathy
crumbled

all that remained
was passion

when he opened
his eyes
the deceit
could not
hide

all that remained
was truth

when he opened
himself
entirely

all that remained
was life

offing

we are caught
in life
and
life is
a wave

sometimes
it roars

bursting free
pushing out
flooding and
submerging us
destroying all
in its wake

sometimes
it whispers
receding
leaving us
baron and dry
gasping from thirst
begging to feel
alive

and sometimes
it breathes
gently

bubbling around us
soothing our skin
the salty sting
healing
our wounds
reminding us
that we are
alive

grow

once it has happened
it is done
and in
the past

the only direction
left to travel
is forwards

Yoga

gayatri mantra

oh but how
can we not
renounce
to such
glory

one must
in entirety
open their mind
to the divinity
within oneself
and within
all life

for it is
this light
and our light

that feeds
the universe

when we open
our selves
to this light
and divinity
we are creatures
no more
instead only
bones and gold

purity and knowledge
will rush through us
eyes open
and the world
is seen
in new
heavenly
light

and so we move
with almighty grace
our actions guided
by supreme
dharma

our minds become
so open and wide
and yet now
we see
only one path

it leads
to the lotus

sage

plant a lotus
in your mind
and
let it open

meditate

close your eyes
even though the dawn is breaking
don't see the light
feel it

feel it within
rising through you
healing
and mending

it is a vein
of energy
pulsing
and vibrating

running through
your core

opening
and releasing

you feel
the light
is gold

you are open
free
and released
it is all
that is left

gold

panglossian

my mind
is soil

it is dark
and heavy

it consumes
rot

and produces
life

rimjhim

like raindrops
life can fall

at first it taps
and dribbles
gently
hitting
your feet

and sometimes
life thunders
a torrent
crashing
and swirling
beneath you

and yet
should you look down

into the water
collected at your feet

what should you see
nothing
but yourself
reflected
in life

for you
are no one else
and can follow
only your self

the droplets
they blur
your vision
until
they do not

and then
you can see
yourself
clearer and truer
than ever before

chai

we are in a melting pot
of brown
so muted
almost nothing
but filled with
everything

first goes the milk
pure and white
and from it we rise
cleansed
it makes
our bones
strong
and our spirit
hard to shatter

grate the ginger
it singes us
in the best way
the zing
makes us feel
so alive

it builds us up
to fight back
at the demons
in our minds

follows the cinnamon
unbroken it steeps
over time
spreading its spice
and goodness
into the surroundings

it adds the musk
and the warmth
and the sparkle

the pepper next
a scattering of bitter
a soft burn

the turmeric follows
healing
from the inside
smiting demons
and lifting the mind

it sinks around
the cardamom
that makes us
dream
the aroma
spinning our minds
into diamonds
and ambition

in goes the red
floral
and powerful
saffron
it brings passion
and fire
golden emotions
tinged with bliss

and of course
we finish

with honey
delicate and sweet
dripping through
the enamoured swirl
coating all
in a thick
sticky
gold

the moon and her children

there are very few beings
that will bare themselves naked
scars and all

and yet she does it
every night
as the sun falters
she lets her sheath of blue slip

her skin is pale
so pale
like skin that has never
felt the sun's passionate kiss

she is marked
scarred
by years of watching

for the worst deeds
always seem to occur
under her watch

but every scar
is a lesson
of how to be human

humans, she thinks
are such profound creatures
so complex

she is simple, she knows
a simple life she lives
every night, she strips and sings
silver-skinned
scars for all to see

but humans, she notices
are her juxtaposition
their lives anything but simple
and their scars
are hidden
deep beneath their skin

and yet
she still feels some interplanetary connection
to these unusual creatures
these beings of skin and bone
bodies made of water and star dust

some say
that she is a mother
and that her children
are the stars

and of course, she laughs
a gentle laugh

the sky twinkles
as the stars laugh with her
for those who think such
could not be more wrong

the stars
feel worlds apart from her
they burn and glow
from within themselves
where she can only
reflect the light
of others

the stars
are perfect beings
golden and glowing
free of scars
and breathing with life

no, the stars are not her children
the people are

they are scarred, like her
they reflect others, like her
and just as she finds her home in darkness
darkness often finds its home in humans

and that is why
she must rise every night

to watch
over her children

laal

it is the colour
of eternity

it sings with
a million voices

it rushes
and gushes
pounding throughout bodies
breathing life
into our bones

it burns and blazes
searing the sky
both morn and eve
drips from a paintbrush
of the one above

it drapes the shoulders
heads and feet
as one steps away from themselves
and joins with another

it mars the pathway
between her hair
a new road
for a new journey

it blesses
the moment a mother
or sister
touches the forehead
of the ones they watch
with their hearts

it is blood
and string
silk
and powder
paint
fire
and love

it is the colour
of eternity

mangalam bhagwan vishnu

he who preserves
we worship
entirely

as he worships
the one
who flies

the freedom
of thought
and self
at peace

the one
whose eyes
are petals

lotus
sweet
able to see
only the
good
and pure

he is the one
we seek
to find
and
to be

antyesti

it so happens
that often
far into life
night falls

it drapes
like a cloak
heavy both
on the one
who is night

and those
around them

to break the night
we burn them
a beacon of orange

of gold
rippling

oh the cloak
is rippling
the heat
and fire
lifting
nocturne

and so
they, the burned one
become the light
in the dark
the embers
in the darkness

and so
every morning
when the sun pervades
the velvet skies
we are reminded
of them

vidhvans

oh, but kali
her yuga
her age

we revel in its chaos
fire and glory

for with destruction
comes a certain sense
of triumph

with rage
comes a strength
a power

lands of rituals and roots
long gone, replaced
with metal and neurons

lands where dharma
has turned to avarice

plains where ahimsa
has blossomed into greed

we must wait
for the white horse
to rage through the flames
and turn one gold
into another

let the fires burn not dharma
but adharma
as the wheel of time
spins once more

with the ivory mane
come the cobalt hands
of kalki

let the stories be true
and let a story unfold
once again

let shambhala collide
with mortal earth
let yoga and humanity
crash together

through darkness
and turmoil
we must grow
akin to a lotus

from the kali yuga
birthed must come
an age
where moksha
breathes on earth

a time
where the only
vidhvans
is the natural collapse
of life
falling from one incarnation
and into the next

acknowledgements

this book is a thank you to everyone

a homage to all who have been in my life. for shaping me and my world

until I could begin to shape myself

Printed in Great Britain
by Amazon